Finger Knitting ①

Handknit projects for kids of all ages

Katsuno Suzuki

Katsuno Suzuki

Born in Niigata Prefecture, Japan in 1944

Suzuki is actively involved in the training of knitting instructors as the founder of the Miyako Lab in Edogawa-ku, Tokyo and the Hagi Lab in Sendai, Miyagi Prefecture. Children need adult guidance to enjoy handknitting projects.

©2002 KATSUNO SUZUKI
Originally Published in Japan by "Hoshi No Wakai" Inc.
English Translation © 2004 by Heian International Inc.

HEIAN INTERNATIONAL INC.
20655 S. Western Ave. #105
Torrance, CA 90501

First American Edition 2004
04 05 06 07 08 09 10 10 9 8 7 6 5 4 3 2 1

Translated by Matthew Galgani
Cover Design by Kathleen Macguire

ISBN 0-89346-939-4

Printed in Canada

Table of Contents

About Finger Knitting

Katsuno Suzuki

Using only our hands and no tools, finger knitting is the base of all knitting. By using our fingers, we create many positive physical affects, including stimulation of the brain and even improved circulation.

Through finger knitting, I've met many wonderful people and had many wonderful experiences. Many visually-impaired people have started with finger knitting, then become quite skilled with crochet hooks and knitting needles. Even if people can't control their fingers as they would like, with a little ingenuity, they can knit many things. The joy of creating is clear to those around them and becomes a powerful incentive.

Finger knitting can be done whether you're young or old, a man or a woman. I hope it will further strengthen family bonds everywhere and increase interaction among us all.

OK...Let's Start
Finger Knitting

- Because finger knitting doesn't use any tools, the stitches are larger than those created when tools are used. The flipside, however, is softer knitting. It's fun to take advantage of that unique elasticity and create many different shapes.

- This technique means you'll be knitting with your fingers. And the thickness and length of everyone's fingers are different. The number of stitches and rows outlined in the diagrams and photos are meant only as suggested goals. Knit using the number of stitches and rows that works best for your fingers.

- For those who have trouble finger knitting or have physical challenges, try a jumbo needle and enjoy knitting that way.

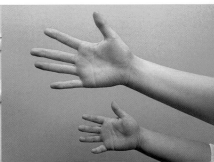

Finger Tube Knitting
Scarfs

Style **B**
See p.9

Style **C**
See p.9

Style **A**
See p.9

Style **D**
See p.11

I knitted it...
Even me!

6

Finger Tube Stitch (4 fingers)

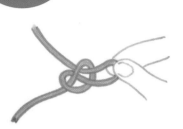

1 Make 1 chain stitch.

2 Place chain stitch on thumb and pull yarn snug.

3 Open fingers, and alternately place yarn, as shown in diagram.

4 Once placed on pinkie, return, placing yarn on areas not yet covered. Bring yarn around to back of hand.

5 Bring yarn around to palm-side, and run over previously placed yarn.

Go to next page →

Finger Tube Stitch (4 fingers) (Continued)

6 Bend fingers, then pull out stitch on pinkie from below and place over pinkie.

7 In same way, place yarn over ring, middle, and index fingers, in that order.

8 Next, run yarn from outside towards you and repeat steps 6 and 7. (The work is created on the back of your hand.)

9 After knitting about 5 rows, remove chain stitch from thumb. (It takes about 5 rows to become stable.)

10 At edge of work, run yarn through each stitch in order, then remove from fingers. Bring end of yarn through outer edge of work to keep from sticking out.

Scrunch fingers together when running yarn. This shortens the length of the yarn and improves the look of your finished work.

Finger Tube Stitch repeats flexible finger movements. This stretching and bending of your fingers improves circulation and stimulates the brain.

Making Scarf: Style A

1 Using finger tube stitch (4 fingers, p. 7), knit to your desired length.

Making Scarf: Style B

1 Using finger tube stitch (4 fingers, p. 7), knit Color A and Color B to your desired length.

2 Bundle what you've knitted, turning it into a group of 4.

<Creating a Group of 4>

Take the string on the left side and bring it in order (from left to right), going over, under, over, etc. to bundle them together.

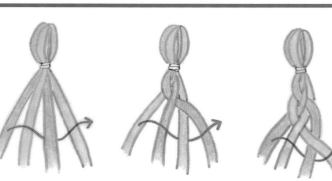

Making Scarf: Style C

1 Using finger tube stitch (4 fingers, p. 7), knit 3 strands to your desired length.

2 Tie all 3 strands with the same yarn, braid them, then tie them again with the same yarn.

3 Add bon-bons to both ends (see p. 31). And you're done!

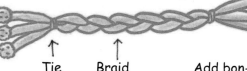

Tie   Braid   Add bon-bons

Finger Flat Stitch (4 fingers)

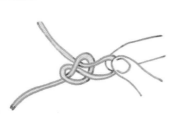

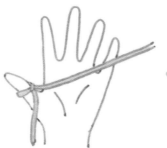

1 Make 1 chain stitch.

2 Place chain stitch over thumb and pull yarn snug.

3 Open fingers, and slip yarn through them as in the diagram.

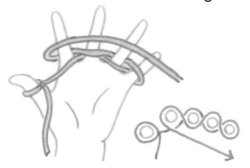

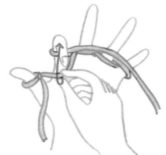

4 Bring yarn around to palm-side.

5 Bend your finger, then take the yarn crossing over from your thumb to your middle finger, and place it on your index finger.

Go to next page →

Finger Flat Stitch (4 fingers) (Continued)

6 Do the same, placing the yarn over your middle, ring and index fingers, in that order.

7 When you've come to your pinkie, bring the yarn around to palm-side. This time, place the yarn from your pinkie to your ring, middle, and index fingers.

8 Repeat steps 5 to 7. Bring the yarn around to palm-side as always, and repeat the steps. (The work will be created on the back of your hand.)

9 After knitting about 5 rows, remove the chain stitch on your thumb. (It takes about 5 rows to become stable.)

10 At the end of the work, run yarn through each stitch in order, then remove from your fingers. Bring the end of the yarn through the outer edge of the work to keep it from sticking out.

Making Scarf: Style D

1 Using finger flat stitch (4 fingers, p.10), knit to your desired length.

* The look and feel will vary widely depending on the wool or yarn you use. Use whatever you like to get the feel you want!

Ooh
How cute...

Yarn Thickness (magnified)
Using 50g alternative yarn

Finger Afghan Knit Scarf

See p.16

See p.16

So light...
and warm!

Finger Afghan Knit

Return→ ~
Start → I   : Afghan Knit

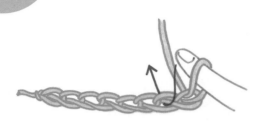

1 Cast on stitch. For the Start, the stitch on your finger becomes stitch1. For the 2nd stitch, go back 2 cast on stitches and insert finger in the chain half-stitch and purl.

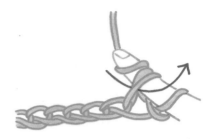

2 Bring yarn from outer side of finger towards you, and pull through as shown by the arrow.

3 Pick up next stitch and pull through in same way.

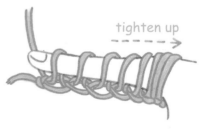

tighten up

4 All stitches have now been picked up. Close gap between stitches and place over finger.

Go to next page →

5 For the Return, place yarn on finger, and pull through as shown by the arrow.

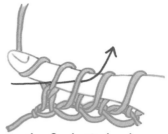

6 From the 2nd stitch, place yarn on finger, and pull through two stitches at a time.

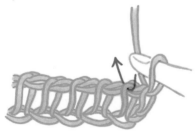

7 You've now returned to all stitches and have knitted the first row. Next, place finger in vertical yarn in previous row to begin Row 2.

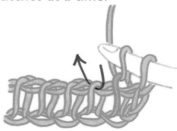

8 Place yarn on finger, going from outside towards you, then continue to knit next stitch.

Go to next page →

In a Finger Afghan Knit, the Return is a chain stitch, so stretching is limited — making it perfect for finger knitting. The work is light, yet warm.

That's a fact.

Finger Afghan Knit (Continued)

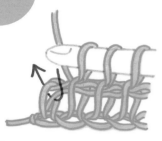

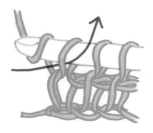

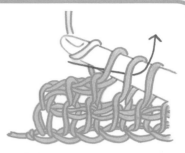

9 For final stitch, take 2 strands as shown in diagram, and pull yarn through.

10 On the Return, in same way as Row 1, place yarn on finger and pull through.

11 From 2nd stitch, pull through two stitches at a time until finished.

Finishing the Work (Casting Off/Slip Stitch)

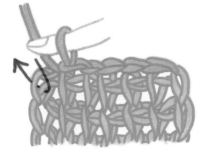

1 Insert finger as shown in diagram, place yarn and pull through once as shown by arrow.

2 Pull through one stitch at a time. At the end, scoop up the 2 strands and pull through, as shown in diagram.

How to Make a Scarf

1 Using a double chain stitch, cast on 12 stitches.

2 Make Top of Beginning stitch, and work straight using Finger Afghan Knit. When finished knitting, cast off.

3 Using finger single crochet (p. 25), knit 2 rows (2 rounds) for outside edges.

Knitted using different material.

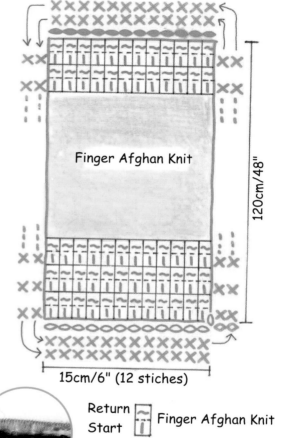

Finger Afghan Knit

120cm/48"

15cm/6" (12 stiches)

Yarn Thickness (magnified)
Using 80g alternative yarn

Return Start

〰 Finger Afghan Knit

⬭ Finger Chain Stitch

✕ Finger Single Crochet

How to Knit Wide Finger Afghan Knits

In a Finger Afghan Knit, you place all stitches on your finger. However, when making an item wider than the amount placed on your index finger, you can knit by also using your other fingers.

In step 4 on page 13, if you run out of room on your index finger, move that stitch to your middle finger. Then knit the necessary width for the start using your index finger, and continue knitting the return. If your middle finger isn't enough, use your ring finger and pinkie to knit the desired width.

Determining Tension

The tension (or gauge) is the ratio of the number of stitches to the number of rows, which forms the base of your work. For every 10cm/4", determine the number of stitches horizontally and, vertically, the number of rows. With the yarn you'll use in your project, test knit 15–20cm/6–8". After adjusting the stitches horizontally and vertically, count the number of stitches and rows within a 10cm/4" area.

Any Finger

Finger knitting is not restricted to your index finger. You can knit using any of your other fingers as well. Be sure to try them all!

Go! Go!

Yarn Thickness (magnified)
Using 80g alternative yarn

Loop-Knitted Scarf

How to Make a Loop-Knitted Scarf

1 Wind yarn around to make a ring with a diameter of about 4 cm/1.6".

2 Inside ring, make 1 finger single crochet stitch, 3 double crochet stitches, and then 1 finger single crochet stitch. (Loop Cast On Stitch, p. 20)

3 Continue by making another loop as in step 1, then inside it, make (as in step 2), 1 finger single crochet stitch, 3 double crochet stitches, and then 1 finger single crochet stitch.

4 Create 8 parts, repeating step 3.

5 Make the 9th loop, and inside that make 1 single crochet stitch, 7 double crochet stitches, and then1 finger single crochet stitch.

6 Next, from the 8th part to the 1st part, repeat 1 single crochet stitch, 3 double crochet stitches, and then 1 finger single crochet stitch.

7 Finish by running through the other piece, created using finger tube stitch (4 fingers, p. 7), and pulling it through the ring.

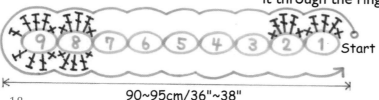

Start

90~95cm/36"~38"

Double Crochet

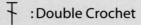 : Double Crochet

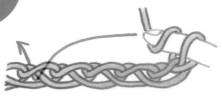

1 On the 3rd Top of Beginning, place yarn on finger, then put your index finger in the 5th stitch area.

2 Place yarn on inserted finger and pull through.

3 Place yarn once more on finger with 3 strands of yarn. Pull out the second strand of yarn found near your fingertip.

4 Next, place yarn on your finger once more, and pull through the remaining 2 strands.

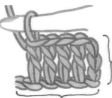

Top of Beginning

Cast on Stitch

5 Repeat steps 2 – 4. When the first row is complete, reverse the 3rd Top of Beginning, and repeat steps 2 – 4.

Loop Cast On Stitch

1 Wind yarn twice around left-hand index and middle fingers.

2 Remove loop from fingers, and place yarn on left hand. Put index finger inside loop, place yarn and pull out.

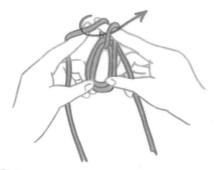

3 Place yarn once more, and pull stitch closed.

4 Loop cast on stitch is complete. (This is not counted as the first stitch.)

5 Put finger inside loop, and pull through yarn.

6 Place yarn on finger as in the diagram, and pull through once.

7 One finger single crochet stitch has now been made. In the same way, put finger inside loop. Now, begin working double crochet.

This knitting is primarily used for casting on stitches, etc.

Finger Chain Stitch   ◯ : Chain Stitch

1 Place yarn on left-hand index finger, holding yarn with middle finger and thumb. Make stitch with right-hand index finger.

2 As indicated by the arrow, place yarn on right-hand index finger.

3 With yarn on right-hand index finger, go through stitch and pull out yarn.

4 As you repeat the steps, you'll create a chain-like knitted stitch.

If you use this double chain stitch in place of a chain stitch cast on stitch, the base stitch will be stronger. It's a perfect cast on stitch for finger knitting.

It's soooooo strong.

Double Chain Stitch

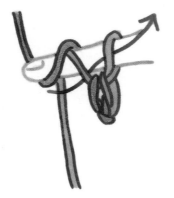

A
Strand close to ball of yarn

B
Strand at 3-times length

1 Using a strand 3 times as long as the length you want to knit, make one chain stitch.

2 Bring the remaining yarn B away from you towards the outside. Bring yarn A from the outside towards you, and pull through as in the diagram.

3 Repeat.

See
p.26

Finger Single Crochet
Hats

See p.30

Finger Single Crochet

X : Single Crochet

1 Cast on stitch with chain. Make one chain on cast on stitch. This is called "Top of Beginning".

2 Skip first stitch of Top of Beginning and insert finger in 2nd stitch.

3 Place yarn on finger and pull through.

4 With both strands on index finger, place yarn and pull through as shown by arrow.

5 Repeat steps 2 – 4. When Row 1 is complete, reverse Top of Beginning stitch, and repeat steps 2 – 4.

How to Make a Hat

1 Make a loop cast on stitch (p. 20), then create 6 single crochet stitches. (Don't knit the Top of Beginning chain stitch.)

2 From the 2nd row on, without knitting the baseline chain stitch, go round in circles increasing the stitches (Single Crochet Increase Stitch, p. 27).

3 On the14th and last row, merge the finger crab stitch (p. 37) and finger chain stitch (p. 22), closing the last stitch with a slip stitch.

Row 14 From the backside of the work, alternately repeat finger crab stitch and chain stitch.

Row 13 No increase/decrease

Row 12 No increase/decrease

Row 11 (30 stitches) + 6 stitches } Brim

Row 10

  ⎰

Row 5 No increase/decrease (24 stitches)   Side crown

Row 4 (24 stitches) + 6 stitches

Row 3 (18 stitches) + 6 stitches } Top crown

Row 2 (12 stitches) + 6 stitches

Row 1 6 stitches in loop

✕ Finger Single Crochet
⟨ Finger Crab Stitch
● Finger Slip Stitch
○ Finger Chain Stitch
⟨ Finger Single Crochet
    Increase Stitch

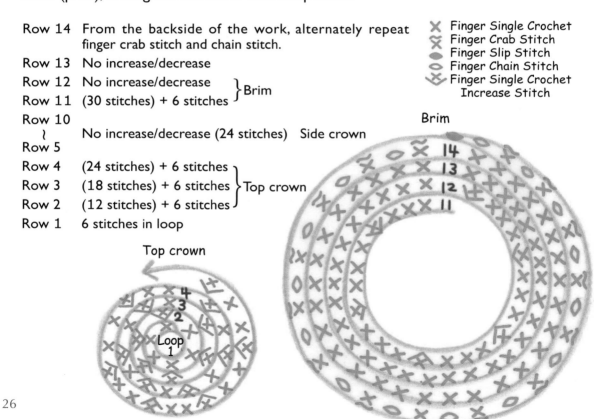

Top crown

Brim

26

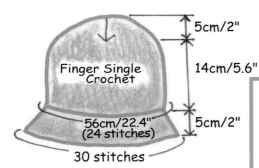

Finger Single Crochet

5cm/2"

14cm/5.6"

56cm/22.4"
(24 stitches)

5cm/2"

30 stitches

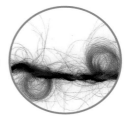

Yarn Thickness (magnified)
Using 100g alternative yarn

Of the different kinds of finger knitting, finger single crochet enables you to make the most detailed work. If you knit using the area around your first knuckle, you'll create consistent and beautiful knitted stitches.

Around here

Finger Single Crochet Increase Stitch

✕ : Single Crochet Increase Stitch

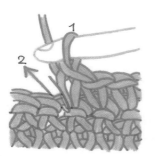

1 Here's how to increase stitches in detailed knitting. In the same stitch, insert the tip of your finger once more.

2 Place yarn and pull through, and work single crochet.

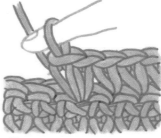

3 On first single crochet stitch, add 2 stitches, and you're done.

Reversible Hats

How to Make a Reversible Hat

1 Cast on stitch (Double Chain Stitch, p. 23) with A color yarn, but not too tight. Try it on for size. (Measure by matching it to your head, then add about 4cm/1.6" to the length.)

2 Knit the first row using finger single crochet (p. 25), then pull the front and back to make a loop.

3 From the 2nd row, don't create a Top of Beginning. Work in circular fashion, without increasing or decreasing.

4 After knitting about 18cm/7.2", end by reducing the number of stitches on the last 3 rows by three-quarters using 2-in-1 slip stitch (p. 29).

5 From the starting point, make a pick up stitch, and knit color B in the same way.

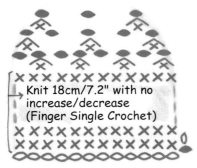

Knit 18cm/7.2" with no increase/decrease (Finger Single Crochet)

Yarn Thickness (magnified)
Using 100g Extra Thick Yarn
(2 colors, 50g each)

Reversible hats laid out

- **⬮** Finger Chain Stitch
- **⬤** Finger Slip Stitch
- **✕** Finger Single Crochet
- **✕̂** Finger Single Crochet Decrease Stitch

* You can change the look further by changing how you knit, so try out many different styles of knitting.

<Example>
Finger single crochet+Finger twisted half double crochet
(p. 25)   (p. 44)

My hat du jour

Single Crochet Decrease Stitch (2-in-1 Slip Stitch)

✕̂ : Single Crochet Decrease Stitch

1 Pull through yarn from Arrow 1, and from Arrow 2.

2 Pass the stitch at the very tip of your finger through the other 2 stitches.

3 The 2-in-1 single crochet stitch is thus complete.

How to Make a Hat (for 2 – 3 year olds)

1 Cast on stitches (38 double chain stitches) and knit 2 rows of finger single crochet. Close by pulling both ends of the second row. (This prevents the stitches from twisting.)

2 Make chain stitch on Top of Beginning stitch, then alternate between finger twisted single crochet (p. 32) and chain stitch. (In the chain stitch of the previous row, work a twisted single crochet.)

3 Once you've knitted 12 rows with no increase/decrease, work 2 rows of 2-in-1 slip stitch. Bind and tie yarn on the last stitch.

4 Knit 1 row (round) of finger single crochet to decorate border.

5 Make bon-bons (p. 31). Make about 20cm/8" of string using finger cord (p. 48).

6 Attach bon-bons and string from step 5 to top of hat. (Work into knitted stitch to join string.)

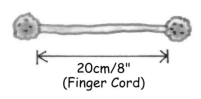

20cm/8"
(Finger Cord)

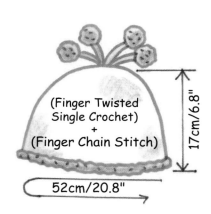

(Finger Twisted Single Crochet)
+
(Finger Chain Stitch)

17cm/6.8"

52cm/20.8"

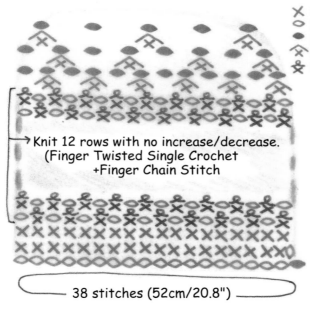

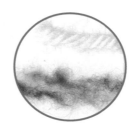

✕	Finger Single Crochet
⌒	Finger Chain Stitch
●	Finger Slip Stitch
✕̂	Finger Single Crochet Decrease Stitch
✖̂	Finger Twisted Single Crochet

→ Knit 12 rows with no increase/decrease.
(Finger Twisted Single Crochet
+Finger Chain Stitch

— 38 stitches (52cm/20.8") —

Yarn Thickness (magnified)
Using 50g Extra Thick Yarn
(Used for bon-bon border
decoration)

How to Make Bon-Bons

Wind wool 50 times around 4 fingers, then tie mid-section
tightly. After cutting the loops on both ends, cut and shape
to make round.

Finger Twisted Single Crochet

 :Twisted Single Crochet

1 Knit Top of Beginning chain stitch. Then insert finger into first stitch and pull yarn through.

2 Twirl finger tip as shown by the arrow to twist stitch.

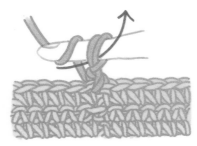

3 Place yarn on finger and pull once through twisted stitch.

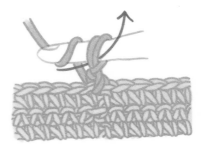

4 Insert finger in next stitch, pull through yarn, and repeat steps 2 and 3.

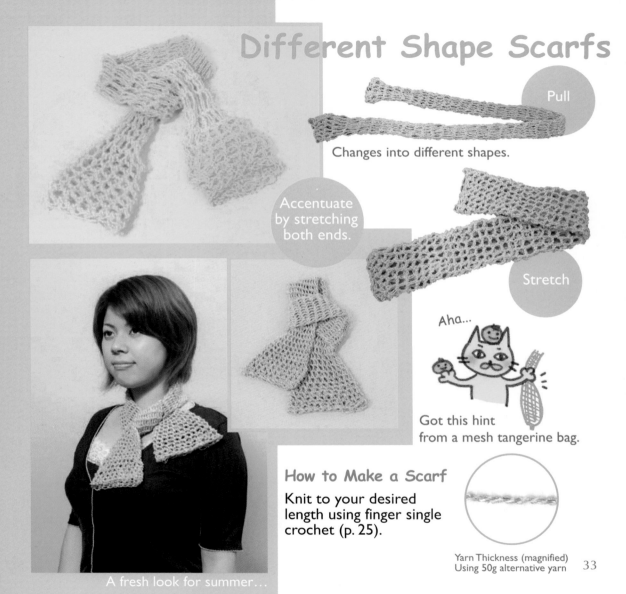

Different Shape Scarfs

Pull

Changes into different shapes.

Accentuate by stretching both ends.

Stretch

Aha...

Got this hint from a mesh tangerine bag.

How to Make a Scarf

Knit to your desired length using finger single crochet (p. 25).

Yarn Thickness (magnified)
Using 50g alternative yarn

A fresh look for summer…

33

Casket-style
Hat

Even with the same hat, how you wear it can change the look.

How to Make a Casket-style Hat

1 From the middle of the top crown, knit oval shape. Cast on 8 stitches using finger chain stitch.

2 While making increase stitches with finger single crochet as per the chart, knit in circles, then set down remaining yarn.

3 After knitting the top, place marker on points A to D, the center front, and the center back.

Go to next page →

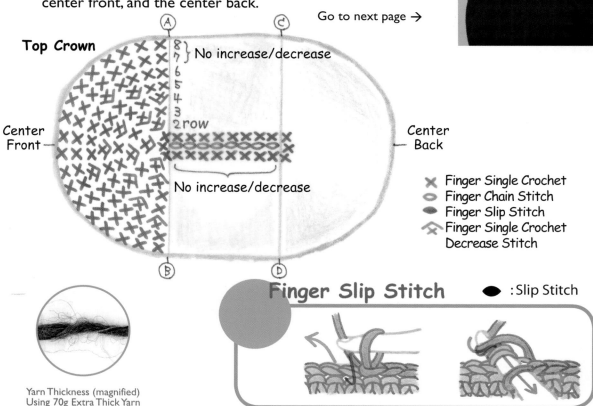

Top Crown

Ⓐ   Ⓒ

8
7 } No increase/decrease
6
5
4
3
2 row

Center Front —

Center Back —

No increase/decrease

Ⓑ   Ⓓ

✕ Finger Single Crochet
◓ Finger Chain Stitch
◖ Finger Slip Stitch
✖ Finger Single Crochet Decrease Stitch

Finger Slip Stitch

● : Slip Stitch

Yarn Thickness (magnified)
Using 70g Extra Thick Yarn

35

4 Place yarn on A, work to B running through center back, then cut yarn.

5 Wind and knit the remaining yarn (on center front, make 2-in-1 decrease stitch), then set down yarn.

6 Slide down 3 stitches from the previous row, place yarn, then work through 2A – 2B, and cut yarn.

7 Repeat steps 5 and 6.

8 Knit 2 brims as in the diagram, then close edge with finger crab stitch (p. 37).

9 Insert support material in between, edge brim (p. 48) to join.

10 Finish by working brim with finger crab knit.

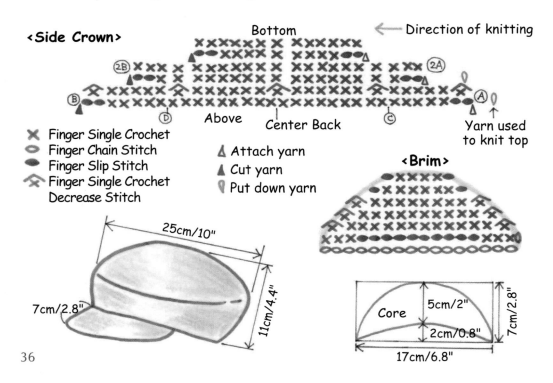

<Side Crown> Bottom ← Direction of knitting

Above Center Back Yarn used to knit top

✖ Finger Single Crochet
⬭ Finger Chain Stitch
⬬ Finger Slip Stitch
✖ Finger Single Crochet Decrease Stitch

⧍ Attach yarn
▲ Cut yarn
❦ Put down yarn

<Brim>

25cm/10"

7cm/2.8"

11cm/4.4"

Core 5cm/2"

2cm/0.8"

7cm/2.8"

17cm/6.8"

Finger Crab Stitch

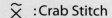 : Crab Stitch

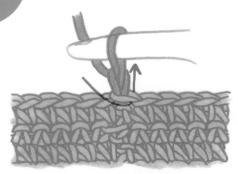

1 Knit1 Top of Beginning chain stitch, then insert finger in slipped stitch.

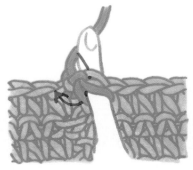

2 Place yarn on finger and pull through as shown by arrow.

3 Place yarn on finger and pull through once.

4 From next stitch, repeat steps 2 and 3. Continue knitting in rightward direction.

Lap Warmer

How to Make a Lap Warmer

1 Cast on 37 stitches.

2 Work 4 rows with finger single crochet (p. 25).

3 On the 5th row, knit 3 finger single crochet stitches. On the 4th stitch, make a double crochet draw stitch from 2 rows down. After that, knit 5 stitches, then make the 6th stitch a double crochet draw stitch from 2 rows down.

4 Until Row 70, alternately knit using finger double crochet draw stitch as shown in the chart. Use single crochet for rows 71 and 72, then close the end using slip stitch.

5 For brim decoration, make 4 fallen pine knitted stitches. (Make 3 finger chain stitches, then work 3 double crochet stitches to same stitches. Insert finger in the edge of the 4th stitch, and repeat.)

Go to next page →

Finger Chain Stitch
Finger Single Crochet
Finger Slip Stitch

Finger Double Crochet Stitch
Finger Double Crochet Front Draw Stitch

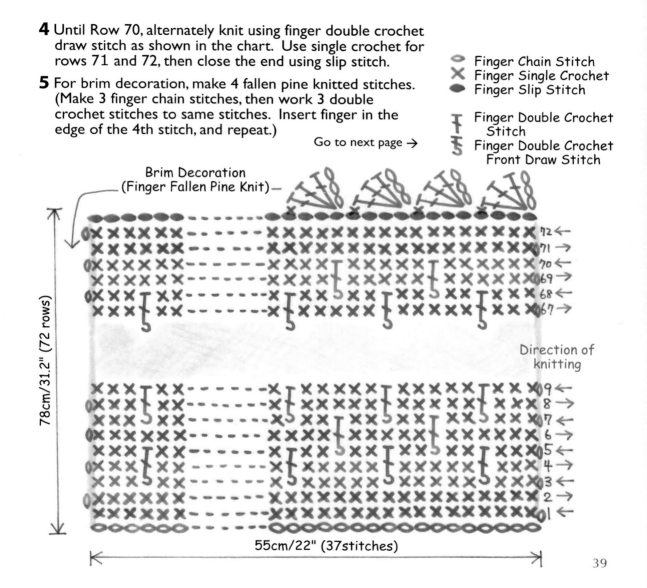

Brim Decoration
(Finger Fallen Pine Knit)

78cm/31.2" (72 rows)

Direction of knitting

55cm/22" (37stitches)

6 Fold over about 17cm/6.8" from the top, and close with yarn/string in two places. The folded area is for inserting your hands.

Warms your hands too!

Finger Double Crochet Front Draw Stitch

⅂ : Double Crochet Front Draw Stitch

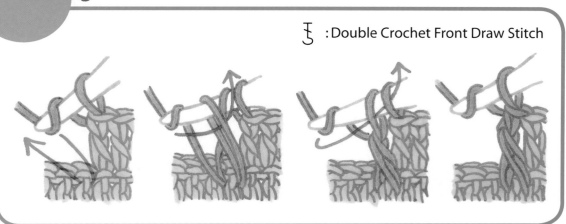

See p. 42

Beautiful Silhouette
6-Corner Stole

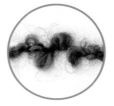

Yarn Thickness
Using 300 - 350g
alternative yarn

41

How to Make a Stole

1 Make 6 finger single crochet stitches inside loop.

2 On the 2nd row, make one finger single crochet stitch, and 2 finger twisted half double crochet increase stitches. Make12 stitches.

3 From 3rd row, make increase stitches in 6 places and knit up to Row 30. At the start of the work, be sure to make an increase stitch, and at the end do not. On Row 31, work finger single crochet with no increase/decrease.

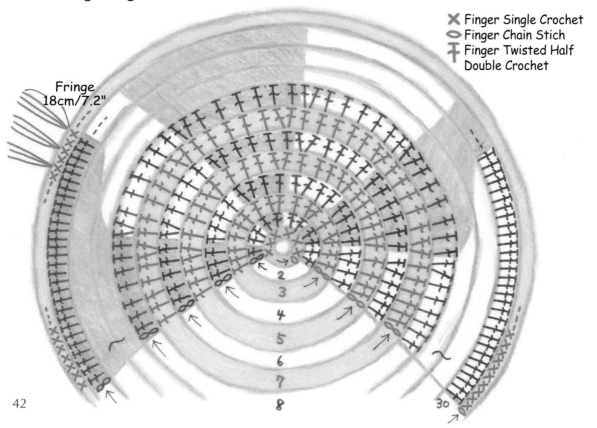

✘ Finger Single Crochet
◠ Finger Chain Stich
† Finger Twisted Half
   Double Crochet

Fringe
18cm/7.2"

42

6 corners will be knitted for this stole. You can knit it to your desired length by adding increase stitches. Therefore, you can make it for anyone, from kids to senior citizens. Keeping track of the numbers as you knit keeps your brain active.

How to Make Fringe

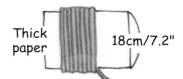

Thick paper

18cm/7.2"

Wind yarn 270 times around an 18cm/7.2" piece of sturdy paper. Cut one end to make 270 strands of 36cm/14.4" yarn. Take this yarn in groups of 3 strands each. Fold each group in half, and join to every other single crochet stitch on the outermost edge of the work.

* Adjust the length of the yarn and the number of winds, depending on the size of the stole, because you'll join 3 strands at a time to every other stitch on the edge.

  Example: An edge with 100 stitches

  100 (stitches on edge) / 2 = 50 (number of stitches to which to attach fringe)

  50 x 3 strands = 150 (number of times to wind)

Finger Twisted Half Double Crochet

1 Make 2 Top of Beginning stitches. Place yarn on finger, and insert index finger in 4th stitch.

$\top$: Twisted Half Double Crochet

2 Twist 2 strands as shown by the arrow to twist 2 loops.

3 Next, place yarn and pull 2 strands through once.

Top of Beginning

Cast on Stitch

4 Repeat steps 2 and 3. When Row 1 is complete, reverse work, make 2 Top of Beginning stitches and repeat steps 2 – 4.

Capes (variation of stole)

30cm/12"

(Twisted Half
Double Crochet)

Edge Decoration
(Finger Single Crochet)

For use with the stole, I made a small cape. In place of the fringe, I decorated the edge using finger single crochet (p. 25) with an alternative wool yarn.

Aaah...

45

Sweater

How to Make a Sweater

1 Knit the back. Cast on 30 stitches. Knit 52cm/20.8" using finger single crochet (p. 25) with no increasing/decreasing. (Leave 2 rows around collar.)

2 Knit the front. Cast on 30 stitches. Knit 42cm/16.8" using finger single crochet with no increase/decrease. Around the collar, knit using increase stitches, as shown in diagram.

3 Join front and back shoulders. From where sleeves are attached, make 26 pick up stitches, knitting 34cm/13.6" with no increase/decrease.

4 Place the front and back over each other, with the outer sides facing each other. Join using slip stitch.

5 Make chain stitch (p. 22), as shown in diagram. Also stitch the hemline of the sweater, as shown in the diagram.

6 Run through the string used to knit the finger cord (p.48) for the collar and sleeve cuffs.

Knitted by Toshiko Sawano
(Tobu Cultural Center)

Yarn Thickness(magnified)
Using 600 - 650g Extra Thick Yarn

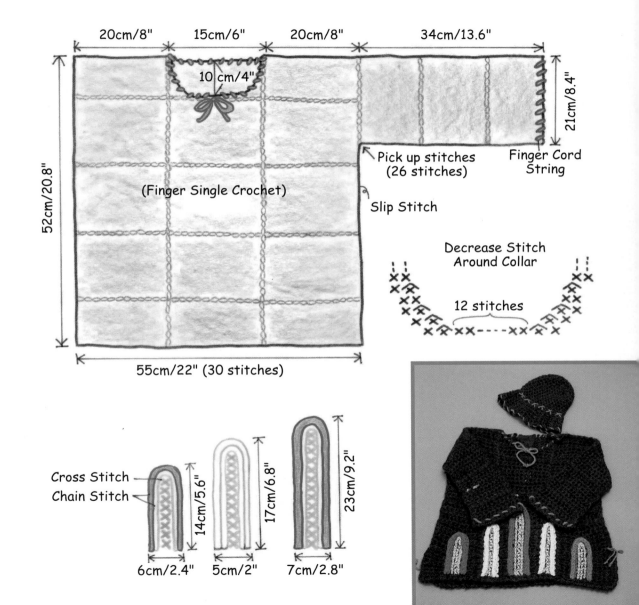

20cm/8"   15cm/6"   20cm/8"   34cm/13.6"

10 cm/4"

52cm/20.8"

21cm/8.4"

Finger Cord
String

(Finger Single Crochet)

Pick up stitches
(26 stitches)

Slip Stitch

Decrease Stitch
Around Collar

12 stitches

55cm/22" (30 stitches)

Cross Stitch
Chain Stitch

14cm/5.6"

17cm/6.8"

23cm/9.2"

6cm/2.4"   5cm/2"   7cm/2.8"

Chain Stitch

The most commonly used method.
Good for curved lines and detailed patterns.

Cross Stitch

As shown below, it allows continuous knitting without cutting the yarn.

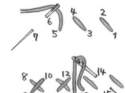

Finger Cord

Method of knitting string for bags, etc.

A — moving yarn B — stationary yarn

1 Make a cast on stitch.

2 Insert right hand index finger into A's loop.

3 Pull through the right-side, stationary B yarn.

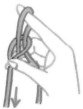

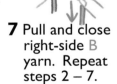

4 Pull out left hand index finger from loop. Pull and close moveable A yarn, held in left hand.

5 Insert left hand index finger in B's loop. Pull out left-side A yarn.

6 Pull out right hand index finger from loop.

7 Pull and close right-side B yarn. Repeat steps 2 – 7.